Spa Fun

Pampering Tips and
Treatments for Girls

Published by American Girl Publishing
Copyright © 2009 American Girl

Questions or comments? Call 1-800-845-0005, visit our Web site at **americangirl.com**, or write to Customer Service, American Girl, 8400 Fairway Place, Middleton, WI 53562-0497.

Printed in China
13 14 15 16 17 18 LEO 10 9 8 7 6 5

All American Girl marks are trademarks of American Girl.

Editorial Development: Erin Falligant, Michelle Watkins

Art Direction & Design: Lisa Wilber, Chris Lorette David

Production: Jeannette Bailey, Judith Lary, Julie Kimmell, Sarah Boecher, and Gail Longworth

Photography page 12: © Kristin Lee/Jupiter Images
Photography page 19: Christopher Zweifel at Quad Photo
Photography page 40, 43: Jim Jordan

Special thanks to Dr. Lia Gaggino, pediatrician; Dr. Vesna Petronic-Rosic, associate professor of dermatology at the University of Chicago; and all of our testers: Alyssa D., Ava D., Erin R., Grace S., Hannah P., Marie S., McKenzie B., Molly L., Olivia S., and Taylor J.

This book is not intended to replace the advice of or treatment by physicians. Questions or concerns about physical health should always be discussed with a doctor, dietician, or other health-care provider.

Cataloging-in-Publication Data available from the Library of Congress.

Dear Reader,

This book is full of everyday ways for you to relax, re-energize, and have fun taking care of your body and spirit.

Tired after a long day of school and sports? Turn to the "De-Stress" chapter for ways to unwind. Feeling blue or bored? Look for ways to rev up in the "Energize" chapter. Want to pamper yourself with special treatments and potions? The "Go for the Glow" chapter is full of spa secrets for your skin and hair. Pamper your friends, too, with a spa party. The "Celebrate!" chapter shows you how.

When you take a moment to be good to yourself, you feel healthier and happier. So what are you waiting for? Open the door, and step into your at-home spa.

Your friends at American Girl

Contents

Get Ready

De-Stress

Go for the Glow

Energize

Celebrate!

Get Ready

Gather a few things, choose your spa spot, and fill it with soothing colors, scents, and sounds.

Stock Up

Materials

Look for measuring cups and spoons, plus a few mixing bowls. Find clean, fluffy washcloths and towels in the bathroom. Gather nail-care tools and a headband to push back your hair. Grab some baby oil, too, which makes a great base for beauty products.

Ingredients

The foods you love to eat make soothing treats for your skin and hair, too. Before taking something from the kitchen, always ask a parent. Here are a few ingredients to have on hand:

- canola or olive oil (Olive oil is great for skin but also expensive. Try mixing half olive oil with half canola oil.)
- plain yogurt
- honey

- oatmeal (the old-fashioned rolled oats—not the quick or instant kind)
- Epsom salts (found at the drugstore) or sea salt (from the grocery store)
- baking soda
- lemon juice (Juice from fresh-squeezed lemons is best.)
- cucumber slices
- vanilla extract

When you see this sign in recipe or craft instructions, ask an adult to help you.

The Patch Test

Your skin may be sensitive to some ingredients, even natural ones. Always test ingredients before slathering them all over your face or body. Dab a small amount on the inside of your wrist, and wait at least an hour to see if your skin starts to burn or itch. If it does, you'll know not to use that ingredient. Wash it off with warm, soapy water.

Set the Scene

Sound Off

Turn off your cell phone and the TV, and turn on a CD of music that soothes you and makes you happy. Or head to your local library to find a CD with nature sounds, such as ocean waves, falling rain, or birds singing.

Do Not Disturb

Hang a "do not disturb" or "gone to the spa" sign on your bedroom or bathroom door.

The Right Light

Turn down or turn off any bright lights. Sit by a window for natural lighting. Better yet, step outside, where you can stretch in the sunshine or sit beneath the shade of a tree.

A Splash of Color

Did you know that colors can affect the way you feel? Find ways to add bursts of color to your spa spot, such as with fresh flowers, a bright towel, or a warm rug.

Follow this color guide to give your spa spot a mini makeover:

Grumpy? Go for green.
It brings peace and restores balance.

Sad? Look for yellow,
which helps you find your smile.

Angry? Try blue—
it mellows and soothes.

Got the blahs? Go red.
It boosts your energy and makes you feel strong and happy.

Scared? Orange
will give your confidence a boost.

Need inspiration? Pick purple,
which will help your creativity kick in.

Quiz
Use Your Nose

1. You can't sleep. It's a good time to reach for
   a. a glass of orange juice.
   b. your lavender hand lotion.

2. You're doing homework, and your energy is
   dragging. You might get a boost from
   a. a stick of peppermint gum.
   b. your vanilla bean lip gloss.

3. You're feeling anxious about tomorrow's test.
   You can calm those nerves by
   a. picking some roses.
   b. sitting beneath the pine tree in your backyard.

Find out which scents calm you down and which ones rev you up.

Answers

1. b. Lavender calms and relaxes you, so it's a great scent to smell before bedtime. Orange and lemon scents perk you up, so save them for morning.

2. a. Peppermint clears your mind and makes you more alert. A stick of gum or a foot rub with minty lotion can be a great study break. Vanilla is calming and can help you unwind *after* your homework is done.

3. a. Actually, stepping outside may help calm you no matter what you do while you're out there, but the smell of roses is especially calming. Pine, on the other hand, stimulates your mind and revs you up.

Make Scents Work for You

Using smells to affect your mood is called *aromatherapy*. Some people practice aromatherapy using *essential oils*—pure forms of plants and flowers. Essential oils can be found at health-food stores and bath shops, but these oils are expensive. You can get the same effects from scented lotions and soaps or with scents from your kitchen or garden.

De-Stress

Feeling stressed out? Here are some ways to relax and keep your cool.

Aah Massage

Oils and Lotions

Choose a lotion with a soothing scent, such as vanilla, rose, or lavender. Or add a drop of vanilla extract to a tablespoon of canola or olive oil. Let the oil sit for an hour to soak up the scent. Before you begin your massage, rub a few drops of the oil between your hands to warm it up.

Healing Hands

Place your right thumb on the palm of your left hand, and your right fingers on top of your left hand. Use your thumb to massage your palm. Gently press and massage the skin between your fingers, especially between your thumb and index finger. Press and hold each fingertip for several seconds. Switch hands.

A Treat for Feet

Rest your foot on the opposite knee. Rotate your foot in circles to loosen your ankle. Rub both thumbs up the arch of your foot, starting at the bottom and moving up toward your toes. Press your thumbs all over the ball of your foot. Gently pull on each toe and massage the skin in between your toes. Then rub your thumbs along each side of your foot. Switch feet, and repeat!

Marble Massage

No time for a full massage? Keep a dish of marbles in your room, and roll your feet over a few of the marbles for a quick foot massage.

Breathe It In

Balloon Breaths

Sit cross-legged. Place one hand above your belly button and the other hand below. Breathe in, imagining that you're filling a balloon with air. Feel your hands rise. Hold the breath for a few seconds, and then exhale. Feel your hands fall as your abdomen presses in to squeeze the air out. Take five balloon breaths.

Mini Meditation

Can you clear your mind for 5 minutes? Set a timer and try. Sit cross-legged with your hands on your thighs. Close your eyes and focus on the sound of your breathing. If your mind wanders, gently bring it back to your breathing. Feeling antsy? That's normal. Meditation is harder than it sounds. But the more you do it, the easier it'll get.

Mantras

Add a mantra to your meditation. A *mantra* is a sound or a word you repeat to help you focus. Think of it as a mini pep talk. Try thinking the words *I am* as you inhale and the word *strong* as you exhale.

What's the easiest way to calm your body and mind? Just breathe.

Nature Spa

Soak It Up

Where better to find calming blues and greens than outdoors? Find a shady place, and spread out a towel or blanket. Lie on your back, staring up at the sky. What do you hear? What do you smell?

Picture This

Can't go outside? Let your mind take you there.
Close your eyes and let your bedroom walls float away.
Imagine that you're lying on a towel in the sand. Can you
hear the waves? Smell the salt water or sunscreen lotion?
Feel the warmth of the sun? Use all of your senses to
experience the scene and melt away stress.

A Private Garden

Zen gardens were first built in Japan out of rocks and
sand. Make a mini version by pouring sand into the lid
of a shoe box. Place pebbles, glass stones, polished
rocks, and seashells into the sand. When you're feeling
stressed, use a fork or chopstick to create designs in
the sand, like currents in water. Want to start over?
Gently shake the lid from side to side.

Soak & Soothe

Bath Basics

Run water into the tub, testing the water with your fingers to make sure it isn't too hot. Close the drain, and add a soother of your choice to the running water. Swish it around. Turn off the water when the bath is half full, and carefully step in. Enjoy the bath for 10 to 15 minutes. Before you get out, turn on the shower to rinse any suds or salts off your skin. Finish with moisturizing body lotion.

Body Soothers

Use your favorite bath-oil beads or crystals, or try one of these:

- 2 cups of powdered milk to soften skin
- 2 tablespoons of rose water to soothe your senses, too
- 1 cup of Epsom salts or sea salt to ease aching muscles

Skin Smoother

Pour 1 cup of uncooked oatmeal in the center of a washcloth. Gather the edges of the cloth and fasten them tightly with a rubber band. Wet the washcloth, squeeze it, and rub it gently across your skin. When you're done, empty the damp oatmeal into the compost bin or garbage disposal (not down the drain!).

Sweet Dreams

A Soothing Routine

After a warm bath or before putting on pj's, slather on a sweet-smelling lotion. Try rose or lavender. Then enjoy a glass of warm milk, or sip some chamomile tea.

A Pillow for Your Eyes

Lie in bed for a few minutes with a lavender pillow over your eyes. Don't have one? Make one. Here's how:

1. In a tall cup, mix 1 cup of uncooked rice with 2 tablespoons of dried lavender (found at health-food stores).
2. Stretch the end of a soft sock over the mouth of the cup. Turn the cup upside down to fill the sock with the rice mixture.
3. Knot the end of the sock, or tie a ribbon tightly around it. Trim the end of the sock with scissors, if you'd like.

Muscle Melt

As you lie on your back in bed, clench your toes for 5 seconds and then release. Work your way up your body, tensing and releasing the muscles in your legs, bottom, stomach, arms, hands, and even face. Then scan your body from head to toe. Is there any tension left, or are you ready to drift off?

Go for the Glow

Try these spa secrets for soft skin, shiny hair, and strong, healthy nails.

Food for Your Face

A Gentle Scrub

Scrubs *exfoliate,* or help your face shed dry skin cells so that your skin glows. For a gentle scrub, mix 2 teaspoons of baking soda with a few drops of warm water. Gently massage the paste over your face in small circles, and rinse with warm water. Treat your face to a scrub once every week or two. (Scrubbing more often might irritate skin.)

28

Moisturizing Masks

Pull back your hair and apply one of these masks to your wet face, avoiding your eyes. Lie back with a towel under your head, and let the mask dry. Rinse after 10 minutes (or sooner if your face starts to itch or feels really tight). Rinse off oatmeal masks with a wet washcloth, emptying oatmeal into the compost bin or garbage disposal.

- Oatmeal-yogurt mask (for normal to oily skin)
  Mix 2 tablespoons of plain yogurt with 2 tablespoons of uncooked oatmeal.
- Honey-oatmeal mask (for dry skin)
  Mix 2 tablespoons of honey with 1 tablespoon of uncooked oatmeal.
- Yogurt-cucumber mask (for sensitive skin)
  Ask an adult to help you purée 2 tablespoons of yogurt with ¼ cup of peeled, sliced cucumber. Use a cotton ball to pat the mask onto your face. (This one is too runny to apply with your fingertips.)

Cool Cucumbers

Have an adult help you slice a cucumber. To soothe tired eyes, place a slice on each eye for 5 minutes. Or sweep a cucumber slice over your face to cool and refresh your skin.

29

A 4-Step Facial

1. Get Ready
Change into your robe, and pull your hair back gently with a headband or ponytail holder. Mix up a scrub and a mask, and ask an adult to help you slice half of a cucumber. Fill a bowl with warm water and another bowl with ice water. Find two clean washcloths, and wrap a towel around your neck.

2. Cleanse & Exfoliate
Press a warm, wet washcloth against your face for a minute to heat and moisten your skin. Then apply a gentle cleanser or scrub, rubbing your fingertips in small circles to cleanse your skin. Rinse.

3. Relax & Refresh
Apply a mask to your face, and set a timer for 10 minutes. Dip a washcloth into the ice water, wring it out, and fold the washcloth into a strip. Lie back, and place a cucumber slice over each eye. Then lay the cool washcloth over the top of the cucumber slices.

4. Massage & Moisturize

When time is up or the mask is dry, rinse it off. Pat your face dry, and apply a small amount of moisturizing face lotion. Make small circles with your fingertips to massage your facial muscles. Then tap your fingers lightly all over your face to bring on the glow.

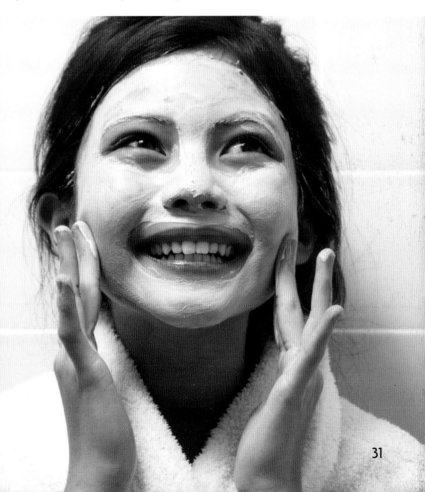

Love Your Lips

Soften

Smooth rough lips by gently rubbing them with a dry, soft-bristled toothbrush—no toothpaste required. Then add a touch of lip balm or gloss.

Shine

Bored with your lip gloss? Try mixing two colors to personalize your shade.

Protect

Did you run out of moisturizing lip balm or gloss? Make your own! You will need:

- 1 teaspoon of beeswax beads (found at health-food stores)
- 2 teaspoons of coconut oil (found at health-food stores)
- small microwave-safe bowl
- food flavoring (such as vanilla or peppermint extract)
- small container with lid (such as a clean, empty lip-gloss container)

1. ✋ Place the beeswax beads and oil in the bowl. Heat in the microwave on high for 1 minute, or until melted.
2. ✋ Ask an adult to help you remove the bowl from the microwave. Stir in 2 to 3 drops of flavoring.
3. ✋ Have an adult help you pour the mixture into the container. Don't cover the gloss or apply it until it is cool and firm to the touch.

Soft Hands & Feet

Finger Soaks

To moisturize your fingers and cuticles, pour ¼ cup of olive oil into a small bowl. Soak your fingers for 1 minute, and pat them dry with a tissue. Want to whiten nails and keep them strong? Soak your fingers for 5 minutes in a bowl filled with 1 cup of warm milk plus 1 tablespoon of lemon juice.

Foot Soaks

Fill a basin with warm water up to your ankles. To soothe tired feet, add ¼ cup of Epsom salts to the water. Or to freshen feet, add 3 herbal mint tea bags to the water. Soak for 5 minutes, and then rinse and dry your feet.

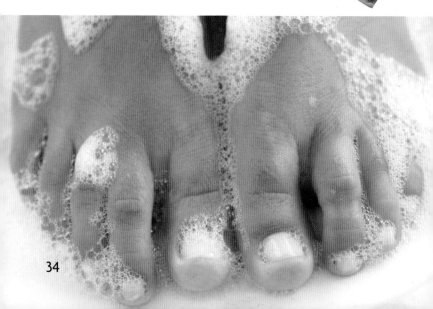

Super Scrub

Soften your hands and feet with this pearly scrub. Combine 2 tablespoons of baby oil, olive oil, or vegetable oil with 3 tablespoons of sugar, sea salt, or Epsom salts. Mix until ingredients form a paste. Rub gently onto hands or feet, and rinse with soap and water. Pat dry. (⚠ Caution: Rinse in a sink or basin instead of the tub. The oil could make the tub slippery!)

Overnight Delight

Massage your feet with your favorite lotion or oil. Then slip into a pair of cozy socks, and let the lotion work while you sleep. You can do the same with hand lotion and cotton gloves. You'll wake up to super-soft skin!

Be Nice to Nails

1. Set Up

Choose a spot near a sink. Read through these 5 steps, and lay out all the supplies you'll need.

2. Cleanse

Still have old polish on your nails? Remove it with a cotton ball and acetone-free nail polish remover. Place the moist cotton ball on a nail for a few seconds, and then wipe the polish off. Repeat with other nails. Wash your hands and nails with warm, soapy water.

3. Trim & Shape

Trim your nails with nail clippers that are about the same width as your nail. Don't cut nails too short—never below the white part. Use a cardboard emery board to smooth out rough edges. Move the emery board over your nails in one direction, not back and forth.

4. Soak & Scrub

Place your fingers in a bowl filled with warm, soapy water (or in one of the hand soaks from page 34). Soak for 5 minutes, and then rub a nailbrush under the white parts of your nails to remove any dirt. Rinse hands and dry them with a towel.

5. Soften

Rub hand lotion or olive oil onto your hands and cuticles. For extra softening, put your hands in plastic bags, and wrap them with a warm, wet towel for a minute or two.

Ready to shine? Turn the page for nail-polishing tips.

Polish & Shine

Polish Pointers

- Roll the bottle of polish between your palms to mix it up.
- Start each nail with a strip of polish down the middle, and add strips on either side.
- Apply a thin coat, and wait at least 5 minutes before adding a second coat.
- Let one hand dry before polishing the other.
- Got polish on the skin around your nails? Dip a cotton swab in polish remover and gently rub off the polish.
- Painting your toenails? Use a toe separator or place cotton balls between your toes.
- Use polish only in a well-aired room, and protect your work surface with newspaper.

Glitz & Glam

Add a bit of fine glitter to a bottle of nail polish, and shake well. Or pour a small pool of polish onto a paper plate and sprinkle glitter over the top, mixing with a toothpick. Now paint your nails, dipping the nail polish brush into the glittery polish.

Sparkly Stones

Polish one nail, and place a flat-backed rhinestone in the middle of the nail (before the polish dries). Repeat with the other nails on one hand. When nails are dry, add a coat of clear polish over the gems. Then do the other hand.

French Manicure

Apply clear polish to your nails, and let dry. Apply white polish across the top of each nail, following the shape of your nail. (If your nails are cut straight across, add a straight line of polish across the tip.) Let dry, and finish with a second coat of clear polish across each nail.

39

Quiz
Hair Helpers

Which statements sound like you?

☐ I *love* my hair-styling products.

☐ I feel as if I have to wash my hair every day to keep it clean.

☐ My scalp feels dry and itchy.

☐ My hair looks dull lately. Where's the shine?

☐ My hair looks oily—even on days that I wash it.

☐ I usually blow-dry my hair.

If you checked any . . .

- blues, you may have buildup from hair gels or sprays. Add a teaspoon of baking soda to a tablespoon of your favorite shampoo. The soda gets rid of gunk and leaves hair super-healthy and shiny.

- greens, your hair may be craving some juice. Squeeze the juice of one orange or lemon into a tall glass of warm water. Shampoo and rinse your hair normally, and then pour on the juice. Leave on for 2 minutes, and rinse.

- reds, try a moisturizing treat. Have an adult help you heat 2 tablespoons of olive oil in the microwave for 5 to 10 seconds, just enough to warm it up. Rub the oil through your damp hair and scalp. Wrap your hair in a towel for 10 minutes, and then rinse hair with warm water. Shampoo your hair, and let it air-dry.

To keep your hair healthy and happy, use these treatments only about once a week. (More often can be *too* much of a good thing!)

It's a Wrap

Wrap It

Choose your favorite conditioner or deep conditioner. Massage it into your damp, towel-dried hair. Then wrap your hair in one of these:

- a shower cap
- plastic wrap
- a warm towel (Throw one in the dryer before you jump in the shower.)

Relax

Set a timer for 10 to 15 minutes, and

- take a bath.
- read a magazine.
- listen to tunes.
- meditate.
- take a mental trip to the beach.
- paint your nails.
- all of the above!

When time's up, rinse out the conditioner, and wash your hair with a gentle shampoo. Let your hair air-dry for shiny, super-soft locks.

Make time to give your hair a little tender loving care.

Energize

Does your mood need a boost? Here are some ways to rev up, recharge, and lift your spirits.

Splash & Spray

Rose-Water Mist

Add 3 drops of rose oil (found at drugstores and health-food stores) to ½ cup of distilled water. Pour into a clean spray bottle. Shake well before misting onto your face and body.

Lemon Body Splash

Squeeze the juice of one lemon into a glass, and add ½ cup of distilled water. Pour the mixture into a clean spray bottle, and shake well. Spritz onto your skin, and follow with an unscented moisturizer. (Heading outside? Hold off on spritzing, as lemon juice can make skin sensitive to the sun.)

Store & Shake

Store your sprays for up to 2 weeks in the fridge, and remember to shake them before each use.

Roses and lemons make these sprays super refreshing.

Scent to Go

Squirt the lemon splash onto a handkerchief, let the cloth dry, and carry it in your backpack. Need to wake up and clear your mind before a test? Pull out your lemon-scented cloth, and inhale deeply.

Greet the day and energize your body with the first few poses of a Sun Salutation.

1. Stand with your feet hip-width apart and your hands together at your chest (as if you're praying).

2. As you breathe in, sweep your arms out to the side and overhead. Lean backward slightly, and look toward the sky.

3. As you breathe out, bend over and try to touch your toes, bending your knees as much as you need to.

4. Breathe in and bring your body up slowly with your arms out to the sides. Bring your arms overhead again and look up. Breathe out and slowly lower your hands back to your chest (palms together).

5. Repeat several times.

You can do these poses any time of day, rain or shine, to wake up your body and mind.

10 Quick
Pick-Me-Ups

1. Drink a cool glass of water with a slice of lemon— or without.

2. Take 3 deep breaths.

3. Smile (even if you don't want to). It tells your brain and body that you're happy.

4. Pop a piece of peppermint gum into your mouth.

5. Give someone a compliment. (The positive energy will boost your spirits, too.)

6. Eat a piece of pineapple or other fresh fruit.

7. Paint your toenails a bright, cheery red.

8. Step out into the sunshine.

9. Fill a vase with fresh flowers.

10. Dance to a rockin' song (or at least listen to it!).

Choose one of these to lift your spirits in 5 minutes or less. Ready, set, go!

Celebrate!

Share your spa secrets
with friends. Invite them
to a party, and spoil
yourselves silly.

Party Prepwork

B.Y.O.P. (bring your own polish)

Let your friends know what you'd like them to bring, such as nail polish, washcloths and hand towels, robes, hair accessories, and soothing CDs.

Spa Stations

Ask a parent if you can set up stations for different spa treatments, such as a manicure bar, a pedicure chair, and a place to do facials (in or near a bathroom). Set out what you'll need at each station plus pillows and magazines for your guests to enjoy in between stations. Choose some music to play in the background.

Cool Treatments

Mix up scrubs, soaks, and masks ahead of time, and refrigerate them until you're ready to use them. Have an adult help you slice up some cucumbers, too. (Remember to have guests test ingredients on their wrists first, especially those with sensitive skin.)

Simple Snacks

Think healthy *and* yummy. Try these:

- Yogurt parfaits. Layer vanilla yogurt with fresh berries and granola.
- Make-your-own trail mix. Let guests fill little dishes with nuts, sunflower seeds, granola, raisins, dried cranberries, and chocolate chips or M&Ms.
- Cranberry spritzers. Pour equal amounts of chilled cranberry juice, pineapple juice, and ginger ale into tall glasses filled with ice.

Secret Stylists

Take turns giving each other manicures, pedicures, facials, and fun hairdos. Throw your names into a hat. When it's your turn for a beauty treatment, draw a name to see who your "stylist" will be!

Laughing Yoga

Sit cross-legged and take a deep breath. Exhale a few times with force, saying "Ha! Ha! Ha!" Did you make each other laugh? That's good—laughing makes your body and spirit feel great. Plus, it's contagious!

Massage Train

Sit in a circle, with each girl gently massaging the shoulders of the girl in front of her. Or pick a partner and give each other hand or foot massages.

Photo Ops

Take before and after photos of your pampered selves—and of all the fun in between.

Spa Souvenirs

Hair Flair

Decorate barrettes and bobby pins with sequins, rhinestones, and small stickers.

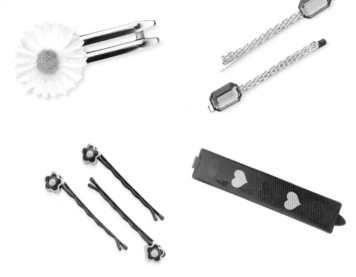

Jewel Jars

Decorate clean glass jars to hold cotton balls, emery boards, and homemade hair and skin treatments. Use glitter glue and nail polish to add sheer color to a jar. Glue on glass beads and flat-backed rhinestones. Tie a ribbon around the mouth of the jar to finish.

Shower Puffs

Make your own sponges.
Each girl will need these supplies:
- 1 square yard of nylon netting (from a fabric store)
- 1 foot of nylon cord
- scissors

1. ✋⭐ Have an adult help you cut each square of netting into 6 long strips, each about 6 inches wide.
2. Stack the strips on top of one another, and fold them like an accordion (starting with the short ends).
3. ✋⭐ Hold the strips in place while an adult wraps the cord around the middle and ties a tight double knot.
4. Tie the ends of the cord together to form a handle.
5. Separate the layers of the sponge as if you were separating the petals of a paper flower. Give the layers a fluff, and presto—shower puff!

Spa to Go

Need ideas for party favors? Try lip gloss, nail decals, travel-sized lotions and shampoos, bath beads, and cute hair accessories.

Kinks & Curls

Bedtime Braids

Spritz hair with water before braiding. Make lots of little braids for really wavy hair or one big braid for gentle waves.

Pin Curls

Twist small sections of wet hair, and wind them into little spirals at your scalp. Pin them in place with bobby pins or hair clips.

Tiny Tails

Separate small sections of hair on the top of your head, and tie them off with little hair elastics.

Morning Makeover

When you wake up, remove the pins or elastics. Don't brush out those waves! Use your fingers to separate and smooth them. Add a dab of hair gel to tame any frizz or flyaways.

Save these special hairdos for sleepovers. Braiding and curling too often can weaken hair.

Are your guests spending the night? As you wind down for the evening, wind *up* your hair.

Feeling pampered from head to toe? Remember to take time for yourself when you need it. You'll be a happier, healthier girl.

Write to us!
Tell us which care tips
you liked best.

Send your thoughts to:
Spa Fun Editor
American Girl
8400 Fairway Place
Middleton, WI 53562

Here are some other American Girl books you might like:

❏ *I read it.*

❏ *I read it.*

❏ *I read it.*

❏ *I read it.*